JAQUI HOLMES

# Productivity Top Tips

*Banish Distractions and Get Things Done*

Copyright © 2024 by Jaqui Holmes

All rights reserved. No part of this publication may be reproduced, stored or transmitted in any form or by any means, electronic, mechanical, photocopying, recording, scanning, or otherwise without written permission from the publisher. It is illegal to copy this book, post it to a website, or distribute it by any other means without permission.

Jaqui Holmes asserts the moral right to be identified as the author of this work.

Jaqui Holmes has no responsibility for the persistence or accuracy of URLs for external or third-party Internet Websites referred to in this publication and does not guarantee that any content on such Websites is, or will remain, accurate or appropriate.

Designations used by companies to distinguish their products are often claimed as trademarks. All brand names and product names used in this book and on its cover are trade names, service marks, trademarks and registered trademarks of their respective owners. The publishers and the book are not associated with any product or vendor mentioned in this book. None of the companies referenced within the book have endorsed the book.

First edition

This book was professionally typeset on Reedsy.
Find out more at reedsy.com

# Contents

| | |
|---|---|
| Introduction | 1 |
| 1 Understanding the Nature of Distractions | 3 |
|    The Psychology of Distractions | 3 |
|    Digital Distractions | 4 |
|    Internal distractions: Overcoming Mental Clutter | 5 |
| 2 Creating a Distraction-free Environment | 7 |
|    Designing a Productive Workspace | 7 |
|    Digital Minimalism: Taming Technology | 8 |
|    Time Management Techniques | 9 |
| 3 Building Habits for Peak Productivity | 11 |
|    Morning Routines for a Productive Day | 11 |
|    Focus-Enhancing Techniques | 12 |
|    Breaks and Downtime – Essential for Productivity | 13 |
| 4 Staying Productive in a Busy World | 15 |
|    Managing Interruptions and External Distractions | 15 |
|    Dealing with Overwhelm and Burnout | 16 |
|    Long-Term Strategies for Sustained Focus | 17 |
| 5 Productivity Tools and Resources | 19 |
|    Essential Productivity Tools | 19 |
|    Recommended Reading: | 20 |
|    Recommended Podcasts: | 21 |
| 6 Conclusion | 23 |
| *Resources* | 25 |

# Introduction

Being productive is key to reaching your personal and professional goals, growing, and making the most of your time and resources. Whether at work or in daily life, staying productive helps you achieve more in less time, leading to greater success, fulfilment, and efficiency. It also sparks creativity and motivation, allowing you to stay on course with your long-term goals while cutting down on stress caused by procrastination or being unorganized.

However, staying productive is becoming harder with the growing influence of technology and distractions. While tech has transformed how we work and communicate, it has also brought along a wave of interruptions. Constant notifications from emails, social media, and apps pull us away from focused work, and the urge to multitask spreads our attention thin, lowering efficiency. The "always-on" nature of smartphones and digital tools also makes it hard to separate work from personal time, leading to burnout and a scattered routine.

On top of that, many digital platforms are designed to keep us hooked, leading to time-wasting habits like endless scrolling and switching between tasks. To stay productive, it is important to manage these distractions by using intentional strategies to focus, set boundaries, and make technology work for you, not against you.

This book is packed with practical tips and strategies to help you boost your productivity and manage distractions. You will find actionable insights and techniques to tackle the modern productivity challenges brought by technology and interruptions. With a mix of psychological principles, time management advice, and practical tools, this book is here to help you take control of your time and stay focused.

# 1

# Understanding the Nature of Distractions

## The Psychology of Distractions

Distractions are a normal part of life, but in today's digital world, they are more common than ever thanks to the endless stream of information and notifications. Our brain's attention works in two ways: top-down attention, where we focus on goals intentionally, and bottom-up attention, which reacts to things happening around us. While the latter was helpful for survival in the past, it now gets hijacked by digital notifications, alerts, and distractions that constantly steal our focus. This makes staying on task harder than ever.

A lot of people think multitasking helps them get more done, but it is actually the opposite. Our brains can't manage multiple complex tasks at once. What really happens is task-switching, where your attention jumps from one thing to another. This "switch cost"—the time and energy needed to refocus—slows you down, increases mistakes, and lowers the quality of your work. Multitasking also drains your mental resources and makes it harder to remember things and perform well.

Distractions and multitasking take a big toll on your productivity, creativity, and overall well-being. When your focus is scattered, you are more likely to miss deadlines and make errors. Creativity takes a hit too because deep, uninterrupted thought is crucial for coming up with fresh ideas and solving problems. Constant interruptions stop you from reaching a flow state, which is key for producing your best, most creative work.

On top of that, distractions add to your stress and can lead to burnout. Trying to juggle multiple tasks while dealing with constant interruptions causes mental overload, which lowers motivation and focus. This can leave you feeling frustrated, anxious, and eventually exhausted, which affects your overall health.

By cutting down on distractions, avoiding multitasking, and focusing on one thing at a time, you can greatly improve your productivity, boost creativity, and support your mental well-being.

# Digital Distractions

While technology brings us amazing benefits, it often takes control of our focus by tapping into our brain's love for novelty and instant gratification. In today's digital world, with smartphones, social media, and apps, we are bombarded by notifications, updates, and alerts. Each one grabs our brain's attention, which is wired to respond to new and sudden things. As a result, it becomes tough to stay focused on just one task when digital distractions keep pulling us in different directions.

A big reason for this loss of focus is our desire for constant connection. Social media, messaging apps, and news feeds are built to keep us hooked, always offering new updates and interactions. This plays into our brain's craving for social approval and fresh information, making us check our devices over and over again. The unpredictability of what we might find (a new message, a "like," a news update) creates a dopamine-driven reward cycle, which makes it even harder to resist these distractions.

Beyond notifications, there are also sneaky timewasters like aimless browsing that can drain our productivity. Many of us casually scroll through social media, news sites, or entertainment apps without a specific reason, often starting with a quick glance that turns into a longer, unproductive session. These small distractions may seem harmless, but they break our focus and make it harder to get back to important tasks.

The overall effect of these digital distractions is huge. Each time we check a notification or get lost in browsing; it takes extra time to refocus on our work. These constant interruptions prevent us from reaching deep, focused work states, which lowers our productivity and creativity. To regain control, it is important to be aware of how technology affects our habits and to set boundaries that help minimize distractions.

# Internal distractions: Overcoming Mental Clutter

Procrastination and perfectionism are two powerful internal distractions that can seriously affect your productivity and well-being. Unlike external distractions, like technology pulling us away, internal distractions come from our own thoughts, emotions, and mental habits. Procrastination often happens because we are afraid of failing, unsure how to start, or just feeling overwhelmed by a task. While putting things off might give short-term relief, it increases stress and anxiety as deadlines get closer, creating a cycle of delaying work and feeling more pressure.

Perfectionism is another big hurdle to getting things done. Wanting everything to be "just right" can lead to overthinking, endless revisions, and difficulty finishing tasks. Perfectionists often procrastinate because they set impossibly high standards for themselves, which makes it hard to make progress. This constant striving for perfection can cause stress, lower self-esteem, and make even simple tasks feel overwhelming.

Stress, anxiety, and overthinking add to mental clutter, making it harder to focus and do your best work. When your mind is full of worries or doubts, it is tough to concentrate and move forward. Anxiety can also lead to rumination, where you keep replaying potential problems or worst-case scenarios in your head, leaving you stuck and unable to take action.

To clear mental clutter and refocus, it is important to develop mental agility—the ability to shift your thoughts, stop overthinking, and approach tasks with a more flexible mindset. Practices like mindfulness and meditation can help you stay in the present, reduce stress, and improve focus. You can also manage perfectionism by using cognitive reframing, which involves focusing on progress and learning instead of chasing impossible standards. Breaking tasks into smaller, more manageable steps and setting realistic goals can help fight procrastination, making tasks feel less overwhelming and lowering anxiety.

By tackling these internal distractions, you will gain more mental clarity, boost your productivity, and reduce stress.

# 2

# Creating a Distraction-free Environment

## Designing a Productive Workspace

Your physical space plays a big role in how well you can focus and get things done. The environment around you directly impacts your mood, concentration, and performance. A well-organized and thoughtfully designed workspace can boost mental clarity and productivity, while a cluttered or chaotic space can create distractions, increase stress, and lower efficiency. The key to creating a workspace that helps you stay focused is to make it both functional and visually pleasing.

Start by decluttering your space. A desk full of unnecessary items can overwhelm your mind and make it harder to focus. By clearing away things you don't need and organizing the tools and materials that are important, you can create a clean, distraction-free area. This not only reduces mental strain but also gives you a sense of control and calm, which are essential for staying focused. Minimalism here doesn't mean getting rid of everything, but simply removing excess so you can concentrate on your tasks.

Setting up your workspace to be comfortable and supportive is just as important. Ergonomics—arranging your space to fit your body's natural posture and movements—can make a big difference. Adjusting your chair, desk, and monitor to reduce strain on your neck, back, and eyes can prevent physical discomfort and fatigue, helping you stay focused for longer periods.

Your workspace's atmosphere also matters—things like lighting, colours, and even scents can affect your focus. Natural light and neutral colours can create a calm, peaceful vibe, while adding plants or personal touches can make the space more inviting. In short, a decluttered, comfortable, and visually calming workspace helps both your body and mind, leading to better focus and higher productivity.

## Digital Minimalism: Taming Technology

Cutting down on digital distractions is crucial for staying focused and getting more done in today's always-connected world. Constant notifications, social media alerts, and entertainment apps can break your focus and make it hard to do deep, meaningful work. To reduce these distractions, start by figuring out which ones are the biggest offenders. Social media apps and notifications are often the main culprits. Turn off non-essential notifications on your phone and computer to resist the urge to check for updates. You can also use app-blockers like "Focus@Will" or "Freedom" to limit your access to distracting websites or apps during work hours.

While technology can distract you, it can also be used to boost your productivity. There are plenty of tools and apps designed to help you stay organized, manage your time, and prioritize tasks. For example, task management apps like "ToDoist" or "Trello" let you break big tasks into smaller steps and set deadlines. Time-tracking tools like "RescueTime" can show you how you are spending your time, helping you spot and fix inefficiencies. Calendar apps like "Google Calendar" are great for planning your day and staying on track.

Managing emails, messages, and calls efficiently is another way to reduce digital overload. Try batching — set specific times during the day to check and respond to emails or messages, instead of reacting to each one as it comes in. This helps you avoid interruptions and stay focused. You can also use email filters to sort important messages, and autoresponders to send quick replies without needing immediate attention. For calls, block out specific time slots for meetings or phone calls, and use "Do Not Disturb" modes to protect your deep work time.

By cutting back on digital distractions and using technology to your advantage, you can create a more focused and productive work environment.

# Time Management Techniques

The Pomodoro Technique, time blocking, and task batching are great ways to boost productivity and manage your time better. They help break tasks down, structure your day, and keep you focused, while prioritization methods like the Eisenhower Matrix and ABC method make sure you are working on the most important tasks at the right time.

The Pomodoro Technique is a simple time management method where you work in short, focused bursts—usually 25 minutes—followed by a 5-minute break. After four "Pomodoros," you take a longer break of 15-30 minutes. This approach helps you stay focused without burning out by giving your brain regular breaks. Working in these intervals helps manage your energy and keep you engaged.

Time blocking means dividing your day into specific chunks of time for certain tasks. Instead of reacting to things as they come, you plan out your day ahead of time, making sure your important tasks have dedicated time slots. This helps you avoid distractions and keeps your day structured. By blocking off time for high-priority tasks, you make sure you are consistently working on what matters most.

Task batching is all about grouping similar tasks together and tackling them all at once. For example, instead of checking your emails throughout the day, you could set two 30-minute slots just for responding to emails. This cuts down on the mental energy needed to switch between different tasks and helps you be more efficient.

Prioritization methods like the Eisenhower Matrix and the ABC method help you focus on the most important tasks. The Eisenhower Matrix sorts tasks into four categories based on how urgent and important they are, so you can focus on what is important but not necessarily urgent. The ABC method ranks tasks as A (high priority), B (medium), and C (low priority), ensuring you are always tackling the most important things first instead of getting stuck on less critical tasks.

By combining these time management techniques with good prioritization, you can streamline your workflow, reduce distractions, and get more done in less time.

# 3

# Building Habits for Peak Productivity

## Morning Routines for a Productive Day

Having a structured morning routine helps set a positive tone for your day by creating a sense of order and purpose. This can lead to better focus, higher productivity, and a clearer mind. When you start the day with a routine, you reduce decision fatigue, meaning you don't waste energy on figuring out what to do next. This not only makes you more efficient but also puts you in a good mindset because you feel more in control of your time and actions.

To create a distraction-free morning, start by cutting out common disruptions like social media, unnecessary notifications, or a chaotic environment. Instead of jumping into emails or scrolling through your phone first thing, try doing activities that boost your energy and prepare you for the day ahead. One way to minimize distractions is by keeping your phone on airplane mode or in another room while you go through your morning routine, so you can fully focus on what is important.

Some key habits for a good morning routine include exercise, planning, and setting goals. Physical activity, even something as simple as a short walk or a quick stretch, can boost your energy, lift your mood, and help you feel more alert. Exercise also releases endorphins, which get your body and mind ready for the challenges of the day. After exercising, take time to plan and set your goals for the day. Reviewing your schedule, prioritizing tasks, and setting clear goals will give you direction and purpose.

Mindfulness practices, like meditation or journaling, can also be great parts of your morning routine. They help reduce stress and improve focus, giving you mental clarity. By balancing activities that support your mind, body, and organization, you can start your day feeling energized and prepared to tackle your tasks.

When you stick to a morning routine that includes positive habits like exercise and goal setting, you lay the foundation for a successful, focused day.

## Focus-Enhancing Techniques

Deep work is all about focusing on demanding tasks without distractions, allowing you to get better quality work done in less time. In a world full of digital distractions and multitasking, this skill has become rare but incredibly valuable. To achieve deep work, it is important to set aside specific time for uninterrupted focus. By blocking out time and cutting off interruptions, you create the perfect environment to get into a "flow" state, where your concentration is at its best and creativity shines. During this time, make sure to turn off notifications, set boundaries with others, and create a quiet, focused space.

Improving your focus can also be helped by mindfulness and meditation. Mindfulness teaches you to stay in the present moment, making it easier to stick with one task without getting distracted. Just a few minutes of daily meditation can sharpen your concentration, building mental discipline and reducing mind-wandering. Simple practices like mindful breathing or a body scan before a deep work session can help ground you and make it easier to resist distractions.

To further avoid distractions, techniques like urge-surfing and setting self-imposed deadlines can work wonders. Urge-surfing is about recognizing the desire to check your phone, browse the internet, or get sidetracked but not acting on it. By noticing the urge and letting it pass, you build up your resistance to interruptions. On the other hand, giving yourself self-imposed deadlines can create a sense of urgency, helping you stay focused. When you set shorter, timed work periods, it adds a bit of pressure that encourages concentration.

By practicing deep work and using strategies like mindfulness, urge-surfing. This is a technique whereby an urge to do something distracting such as checking your email is recognised but ignored. When the urge subsides, refocus and move on. This builds self-control, and urges become less strong over time as you learn to manage them. Setting self-imposed deadlines is also helpful. By combining these techniques, you can greatly improve your focus, resist distractions, and get important tasks done more efficiently and effectively.

## Breaks and Downtime – Essential for Productivity

The science behind taking breaks shows that rest is essential for staying productive because our brain and body have limits when it comes to sustained focus and energy. Research has found that working non-stop for long periods can lead to mental fatigue, reduced concentration, and lower productivity. Taking breaks helps prevent burnout, refreshes your mind, and restores focus, so you can perform better for longer stretches of time.

Active breaks, like walking, stretching, or doing light physical activity, are especially good for both your body and mind. These activities get your blood flowing, improve your posture, and send more oxygen to your brain, which boosts alertness and creativity. For example, a quick walk outside not only gives your eyes a break from screens but also clears your mind by being in nature. Stretching can release muscle tension, ease discomfort, and even lift your mood, making it easier to focus when you get back to work.

On the other hand, passive breaks—like scrolling through social media—can be less helpful. While they may offer a short distraction, they can overload your mind with extra information and leave you feeling even more drained. Instead of recharging, these activities often use the same mental energy you need for work, making it harder to regain focus.

The idea of the 90-minute work cycle is based on the body's natural energy patterns, called ultradian rhythms, which control periods of alertness and fatigue. Studies suggest that after about 90 minutes of focused work, our ability to concentrate starts to fade. Taking a break after this period allows your brain to rest and recharge. Short, restorative breaks—whether active or simply relaxing—help reset your mental energy, making your next 90-minute work session more effective.

By balancing work with restorative breaks, especially active ones, you can boost your productivity, improve focus, and avoid burnout.

# 4

# Staying Productive in a Busy World

## Managing Interruptions and External Distractions

Dealing with interruptions from colleagues, family, or friends can be tough, especially when you are working from home or in open offices. These interruptions can break your concentration, making it harder to get things done. The key to managing them is setting clear boundaries, letting people know when you need to focus, and learning to say no—without feeling bad about it.

First, set boundaries with the people around you. Let them know when you are available and when you need uninterrupted time to work. For example, if you are working from home, establish specific hours when you should not be disturbed unless it's urgent. In an office, you can use simple signals like wearing headphones or closing your door to show that you are focused and do not want to be interrupted.

Next, communicate your needs. Talk to your colleagues, friends, or family members about your work habits. Let them know that you get the most done when you can focus without distractions for a while. It is helpful to explain that you appreciate their requests but need dedicated focus time to complete important tasks.

One of the harder parts is learning to say no without feeling guilty. Many people struggle with this because they don't want to seem rude or unhelpful. But saying no is important for protecting your time. You don't have to be harsh about it—try saying things like, "I'm working on something important right now; can we talk later?" or "I'd love to help, but I'm focused on a deadline." This way, you are being polite but still keeping your focus.

By setting boundaries, clearly communicating your needs, and learning to say no when necessary, you can stay productive while keeping positive relationships with the people around you.

## Dealing with Overwhelm and Burnout

Recognizing when you feel overwhelmed or burned out is key to staying productive and taking care of yourself in the long run. Burnout often shows up as constant tiredness, trouble focusing, irritability, and feeling disconnected from your work. Before burnout happens, you might feel overwhelmed, which can feel like being mentally stuck, stressed by a long to-do list, or anxious about not meeting expectations. If you ignore these signs, it can seriously affect your performance and health, so it is important to tackle them early.

One way to manage stress and your workload is by prioritizing tasks. Tools like the Eisenhower Matrix can help you sort tasks by urgency and importance, so you focus on what is most important first and delegate or delay less urgent tasks. Breaking big tasks into smaller, more manageable steps also helps reduce overwhelm, making it easier to see progress. Time blocking—where you schedule specific time for each task—can add structure to your day and prevent you from taking on too much at once.

To ease feelings of overwhelm, stress-relief techniques like mindfulness, meditation, or simple breathing exercises can help. Even a short mindfulness session can calm your mind and reduce stress hormones. Physical activity, such as walking or some stretching, can also lower stress by releasing endorphins and lifting your mood.

Balancing work with self-care is crucial to avoid burnout. Being productive doesn't mean working nonstop; it is also about knowing when to rest. Make sure to take regular breaks, schedule longer rest periods during the week and do things that recharge you—whether that's reading, exercising, or spending time with loved ones. Getting enough sleep is also super important for staying focused and energized.

In short, staying productive means balancing your work with self-care. Listen to your body, manage your tasks wisely, and make time for rest. This approach helps you stay successful and avoid burnout in the long term.

## Long-Term Strategies for Sustained Focus

Building a personal productivity system that works for the long-haul means creating a flexible approach that can change as your needs and circumstances do. While popular methods like the Pomodoro Technique or time blocking are great starting points, the real secret to long-term success is customizing them to fit your unique lifestyle, work habits, and goals.

Start by figuring out when you are most productive during the day, understanding your work style, and outlining your main responsibilities. This will help you build a structure that plays to your strengths. Use tools like task managers, calendars, or note-taking apps to keep yourself organized and make it easier to prioritize tasks. A good productivity system also includes a balance between work and rest, making sure you take breaks to avoid burnout.

As life changes—whether it is new responsibilities, a career shift, or personal growth—your productivity system should evolve with you. It is important to adjust your environment and habits to stay efficient as these changes happen. For example, if you switch from working in an office to working from home, you may need to tweak your routines, set up a more focused workspace, or create clearer boundaries with family. Likewise, if your personal priorities change, like needing more time for self-care or family, you will need to rework your schedule to reflect that. Flexibility is key to making sure your system keeps supporting your goals, no matter how they shift.

Another crucial part of maintaining your system is regular reflection and review. Checking in on your system weekly or monthly allows you to see what is working, what's not, and where you can improve. You can assess your progress toward goals, spot any bottlenecks, and think about adjustments that will help. By fine-tuning your time management techniques and daily routines as you go, you will stay adaptable, focused, and productive in the long run.

In short, a personal productivity system works best when it is tailored to you, flexible, and constantly evolving to meet your changing needs.

# 5

# Productivity Tools and Resources

## Essential Productivity Tools

In today's digital world, there are tons of apps and tools that can help you organize tasks, manage projects, and block distractions, making it easier to work efficiently. These tools not only boost productivity but also help you stay organized and focused in both your personal and professional life. The key is finding the right mix of digital and analogue tools that work best for your style.

For task and project management, apps like Trello, Asana, and Todoist are popular choices. Trello uses a simple board system where you can organize tasks into categories, making it easy to see your progress at a glance. Asana is great for teams, with features that let you collaborate, set deadlines, and track workflows. Todoist is excellent for personal task management, offering easy-to-use to-do lists and tools to prioritize your tasks.

To block distractions, tools like Freedom, RescueTime, and Focus@Will can keep you on track. Freedom lets you block distracting websites and apps across all your devices for a set period. RescueTime monitors how you spend your time online and gives you insights into your productivity. Focus@Will uses music designed to improve concentration, helping you focus while you work.

If you are looking to build better habits and manage your time, apps like Habitica and Streaks can help. Habitica turns habit-building into a game, rewarding you for completing tasks and sticking to good habits. Streaks is a simple app where you can track daily habits and stay motivated by maintaining streaks of completed tasks.

While digital tools offer a lot of structure and convenience, some people prefer using analogue methods like paper planners or bullet journals. Writing tasks by hand can help with remembering them and gives you a satisfying feeling when you cross off completed items.

In the end, the best system for you depends on your personal preferences and how you like to work. Some people thrive with digital tools, others prefer the hands-on experience of analogue methods, and many find a mix of both works best.

## Recommended Reading:

For those of you who would like to dive more deeply into some of these topics, here is a list of recommended reading and podcasts on a range of topics that will help to deepen your knowledge of the subjects covered and support your further skills development.

1. "Deep Work" by Cal Newport
2. Focuses on the value of undistracted, focused work and how to cultivate this ability in a world full of distractions.
3. "Atomic Habits" by James Clear
4. Offers a deep dive into habit formation, providing practical strategies for building good habits and breaking bad ones.
5. "The 7 Habits of Highly Effective People" by Stephen Covey

6. A classic book on personal development, it outlines key principles for becoming more effective in both personal and professional life.
7. "Getting Things Done: The Art of Stress-Free Productivity" by David Allen
8. Introduces the GTD (Getting Things Done) system, a widely used method for organizing tasks and managing projects efficiently.
9. "Essentialism: The Disciplined Pursuit of Less" by Greg McKeown
10. Focuses on simplifying your life by focusing on what truly matters, encouraging you to eliminate unnecessary tasks and distractions.
11. "The Power of Habit" by Charles Duhigg
12. Explores the science behind habits and how they influence our lives, offering insights into changing behaviours for greater productivity.
13. "Make Time: How to Focus on What Matters Every Day" by Jake Knapp and John Zeratsky
14. Provides a simple framework for structuring your day to focus on what matters most, while avoiding distractions and busyness.
15. "The One Thing" by Gary Keller and Jay Papasan
16. This book emphasizes the importance of focusing on the single most important task to maximize productivity and achieve extraordinary results.

## Recommended Podcasts:

1. "The Tim Ferriss Show"
2. Tim Ferriss interviews top performers from various fields, exploring their productivity habits, routines, and strategies for success.
3. "The Productivity Show" by Asian Efficiency
4. Focuses on actionable tips and strategies to boost your productivity, including time management techniques and personal development.

5. "Beyond the To-Do List" by Erik Fisher
6. Features interviews with productivity experts who share their insights and strategies on how to work smarter and achieve goals.
7. "Deep Questions with Cal Newport"
8. Hosted by Cal Newport, this podcast dives into topics related to deep work, focus, and living a more meaningful and productive life.
9. "Hurry Slowly" by Jocelyn K. Glei
10. Explores how to achieve more by doing less, discussing strategies for finding balance, managing burnout, and focusing on what matters most.
11. "The Focused Podcast" by David Sparks and Mike Schmitz
12. A podcast that helps you learn how to better focus your time, energy, and attention on truly important things.
13. "The Daily Stoic" by Ryan Holiday
14. Although not solely about productivity, this podcast applies Stoic philosophy to modern life, teaching you how to manage time, handle distractions, and build resilience.

These books and podcasts offer valuable insights for enhancing productivity, managing time effectively, and optimizing focus, making them excellent resources for productivity enthusiasts. You will also find some additional books and online materials in the 'Resources' section of the book below.

# 6

# Conclusion

This book is a guide to tackling the everyday challenges that stop us from being our most productive selves. These challenges affect both our work and personal lives. With only 24 hours in a day, it can feel overwhelming to meet our goals, especially in a world full of distractions designed to slow us down and mess with our plans. By understanding the root of these issues, we can develop strategies to take back control.

There's no one-size-fits-all solution, but here are some key actions that can help you improve:

1. Take a look at your workspace and see if there are ways to make it better.
2. Build a distraction-free morning routine, including turning off social media and silencing your phone.
3. Plan your day in time blocks, with breaks after every 90 minutes of focused work. Don't forget to set specific times for handling emails!
4. Group similar tasks together to knock them out at once.
5. Focus on what's most important and prioritize those tasks.

6. Communicate with family and coworkers to get their support in minimizing distractions.

Each step you take will help make things a little better, but remember, everyone is different. Some techniques might work better for you than others. Celebrate your wins and keep reflecting on how you can make things even better!

I hope you have enjoyed this book. If you found it helpful, I would be very appreciative if you leave a favourable review on Amazon! Thank you.

# Resources

Allen, D. (2001). Getting Things Done: The Art of Stress-Free Productivity. Retrieved October 15th 2024, from http://ci.nii.ac.jp/ncid/BA74888857

Carroll, R. (2021). The Bullet Journal Method: Track Your Past, Order Your Present, Plan Your Future. Fourth Estate.

Charnas, D. (2017). Everything in its place: The Power of Mise-En-Place to Organize Your Life, Work, and Mind. Rodale Books.

Cirillo, F. (2018). The Pomodoro Technique: The Acclaimed Time-Management System That Has Transformed How We Work. Crown Currency.

Clear, J. (2022). Atomic habits. Editura Trei SRL.

Covey, S. R. (2004). The 7 Habits of Highly Effective People: Powerful Lessons in Personal Change. Simon and Schuster.

Crenshaw, D. (2021). The myth of multitasking: How "Doing It All" Gets Nothing Done. Mango Media Inc.

Duhigg, C. (2012). The power of habit: why we do what we do in life and business. Retrieved October 15th 2024, from https://ci.nii.ac.jp/nc

id/BB17363429

Dweck, C. (2007). Mindset: The New Psychology of Success. Random House.

Elrod, H. (2023). The Miracle Morning (Updated and Expanded Edition): The 6 Habits That Will Transform Your Life Before 8 AM. John Murray One.

Eyal, N. (2019). Indistractable: How to Control Your Attention and Choose Your Life. Bloomsbury Publishing.

Fiore, N. (2023). The now habit: A Strategic Program for Overcoming Procrastination and Enjoying Guilt-Free Play. Random House.

Grenny, J., McMillan, R., & Switzler, A. (2002). Crucial conversations: tools for talking when stakes are high. Retrieved October 15$^{th}$ 2024, from http://ci.nii.ac.jp/ncid/BB08235712

Hunter, H. (2022). Stop Overthinking! 9 steps to Eliminate stress, anxiety, negativity and focus your productivity. Juran Publications

Johnson, A., & Proctor, R. W. (2004). Attention: Theory and Practice. SAGE.

Jones, A. (2015). 10% happier: How I tamed the voice in my head, reduced stress without losing my edge, and found self-help that actually works D Harris. Qualitative Social Work, 14(2), 295–297. Retrieved October 15$^{th}$ 2024, from https://doi.org/10.1177/1473325015571211a

Keller, G., & Papasan, J. (2014). The One Thing: The Surprisingly Simple

## RESOURCES

Truth Behind Extraordinary Results: Achieve your goals with one of the world's bestselling success books. John Murray One

Loehr, J., & Schwartz, T. (2006). The power of full engagement. Managing energy, not time, is the key to high performance and personal renewal. In Gabler eBooks (pp. 199–216). Retrieved October 15th 2024, from https://doi.org/10.1007/978-3-8349-9251-2_17

McKeown, G. (2014). Essentialism: the disciplined pursuit of less. Retrieved October 15th 2024, from http://ci.nii.ac.jp/ncid/BB18123216

Newport, C. (2016). Deep work: Rules for Focused Success in a Distracted World. Hachette UK.

Tolle, E. (1997). The Power of Now: A Guide to Spiritual Enlightenment. Retrieved October 15th 2024, from http://ci.nii.ac.jp/ncid/BA56671795

Tracy, B. (2017). Eat that frog. Mango Media Inc.

Vanderkam, L. (2018). Off the Clock: Feel Less Busy While Getting More Done. Hachette UK.

www.ingramcontent.com/pod-product-compliance
Lightning Source LLC
Chambersburg PA
CBHW070958220526
45471CB00007B/3092